Fall Risk

Sept 2021

*To Chloë
my love!*

*love,
mom*

*Always keep writing
I love you*

poems by

Stacey Z Lawrence

Finishing Line Press
Georgetown, Kentucky

Fall Risk

Publisher: Leah Huete de Maines
Editor: Christen Kincaid
Cover Art and Design: Ted Rall
Author Photo: Stacey Z Lawrence

Order online: www.finishinglinepress.com
also available on amazon.com

Author inquiries and mail orders:
Finishing Line Press
P. O. Box 1626
Georgetown, Kentucky 40324
U. S. A.

Table of Contents

NEW

ACKNOWLEDGEMENTS

For Mark C G Lawrence

& give me my memories/how i waz when i waz there
—Ntozake Shange

Keeping You

I promised you
that morning in your office, legs resting on a desk
we built from a wooden door etched in
hearts & arrows
        ML+SL
pink still in your wink,
you had a few months more,

so now I write
inhaling you poem after poem they come & come like
ticker-tape parades, Rapunzel's hair, Isadora Duncan's red scarf
waving underneath your cloud
I wait for rain beneath sun-drenched cumulus
that only pours in echoes.

OLD

Zip

I notice you first
at the college playhouse
black & white headshots of
actors hang crooked. Tall &
spindly in faded Levis, leather
brogues, Marlboro
dangles from that lower lip
on tiptoe we kiss, you hold me
in a clumsy hug. Hungry
we scuttle into your Sentra,
steer under golden arches
demanding burgers, rings, shakes.
Slurping & greasy fingered
we pop in a Nirvana cassette,
Cobain laments
as the freeway whizzes zippy
below our soles.

Fringes

I am 19 &
sneak out of the sanctuary
with you
during some rabbi's sermon,
we search for trouble, find Manischewitz
& guzzle dixies, giggling through front doors
like 3rd graders in June. Arms topped with soft tallit,
we toss sneakers like lost grenades onto
our little beach, rest borrowed prayer shawls
in damp sand, kiss silent under stars
as holy fringes tickle our skin.

חי

Following her cue, I slide along
the pew & kneel onto a retractable leather
hassock that falls
with the pound of a judge's gavel.
Unlike me, your mum
crosses her chest
kisses her crucifix & mumbles something
about god. She looks so cool, so "Magdalene."
Soon a central line swells
as young & old
take communion,
devouring stale wafers like imported Camembert.
During the sermon a basket crawls
across collected laps, I drop in a dollar &
slip my Chai
deep underneath my shirt.

Radio City

This morning my grandmother is
wholly wrapped in a sandy
polyester pantsuit, gulps black
coffee straight like a shot, skims the
Newark Star-Ledger where she tells us

they had a four-story walk-up
above my grandfather's delicatessen on
Ferry Street where she collected change
& dumped striped mints into a blue
bowl, linger of kosher salami in
ginger curls she
scrubbed the sink, iron-willed

just as she was
one glorious year
trotting across a midtown stage
legs brushing velvet curtains,
T-strap shoes, paid
to don red lipstick and
kick fiercely.

Prelude to a Ferry Crossing

Our sapphire pipe sparkles
lighting up
winding road, beacon for cops
as small clouds ascend
our sunroof, flip-flops rest on
the dash I inhale deep & free
gaze at the view
beyond you,

gingerbread houses beneath
slices of lapis lazuli
where sails wave like
white envelopes in December.
Seagulls clump & gather
behind fish trucks
& busses like radio flyers
shuttle holiday flock into that
bakery. I buy two coffees, crusty bread
rest my feet on your knees in
our windowless nook
& behold.

Christmas in England

Smoggy in a sunny mini
your gran is late but slips in next to
her favorite,
kisses vintage jokes in your ear
as the kitchen sings with Brits
cackles harmonize like bees
under the BBC
ladies bang dishes & scrape plates
as we stretch like cats lapping Malbec.

The first course
travels gently onto emerald linen,
silverware glints like dinoflagellates
in a dark lagoon. By the cheese course
drunken elbows kneel into
crumpled paper crowns
abandoned for cream tea
& ginger biscuits in the lounge.

Meanwhile, jetlagged & in love,
we hide like brown paper packages,
your leg deep around
my hip my smile near your lips
& laugh at ugly ski socks that
yawn at bed's edge.

The Farm

My grandfather
hunches above worn
baskets, August sun at his shoulders, bushels at his feet
he is the master juggler & sifts
beefsteaks from brandywines as if
ornamental relics from god, until
evening falls when the farmer
rocks to the crickets song,
cotton curtains billow in soft summer gloaming
exposing that view where

in thirty years
a Walmart moves in
tomatoes sprinkled with benzoic acid,

but for now, we see him sway

toing & froing
cheap whisky in his grip, turbid
pulp wedged
beneath a farmer's fingernails.

Skiing with Mr. Z

They call him Mr Z,
freckled skin like a
raw peach.

Each winter
two yellow busses
roar onto a school blacktop where
kids wait with ski
boots & backpacks, middle schoolers
chant his name as he
dances aboard like some
prime time talk show
host, mechanically
shifting his limbs.
He calls this, "The Robot."

Accustomed to his antics
you & my sister & me
avert our eyes
sitting hidden,
just behind the driver,
(also chanting for my dad.)

At pick-up
parents are late, crash on
an icy highway.
We wait in a lonely cafeteria
& slope like moguls across linoleum.
Everyone complains,

except Mr. Z
who shares riddles
& equations, even
tutors a covey of 7th graders.

It is quiet now, his students
are gone. Just a black sky

shivering under a few stars.
Hampered with gear the four of us
laugh at our load
and together
"Robot"
out into the snow.

Portrait

Bolting from that word
the cop tears after him
across a Buy-Rite parking lot
& highway barrier, the man
hastens his pace
ignores untied lace
wipes his face
climbs a chain fence
but falls hard

       Black skin pounds
on haggard cement but
like a balloon, broken breath
inflates the man,
only to be whipped by
some pig's pistol
deep within the crevice of his skull.

The week of trial, cross-legged in a grey suit
you digest thousands of pages
spread across our
kitchen floor like millions of
pick-up sticks.

The courtroom is long & looming
(a little like you, my Love)
with an ivory ceiling etched in gold. You advocate
under glass candelabras that highlight
portraits of White men in Black frames
where you object & object
pounding your fists, my quiet husband,
for justice.

High

I pour tea over
cream
Stir my rum, fungus
gleams
Above green sprouting
seas
We tend in attic,
bees
You course through leafy
trees

Pluck a plump one &
grind
Lingering notes, sweet
pine
We nuzzle close, blood-
line
Pass pipe beneath moon
shine
I gawk at our green-
mine

Cold tea we sip &
kiss
This life of utter
bliss
We avoid kitty
piss
Grow, laugh & rem-
inisce
Dream about future
kids

Lay my head on your
lap
Glance to a beige torn
map

Tug at your black wool
cap
You run through me like
sap
as we drift, soft long
nap

Red-Nosed

I follow the light of your ciggy
through the damp stinky lodge where
after a day dancing on Black Diamonds
we peel off socks like overripe banana skins
lay the fruit by the hearth & kiss & sip whisky
from the silver flask I gave you,

my first Christmas in England
when your dad pretends to be Santa Claus &
ho-ho-hos from room to room
in that storybook house
bestowing striped peppermint candy to
gathered kin as I search & search
slurping on sugar

you skip sweets
& instead light up
on the thatched roof
where I finally find

my Rudolph.

BORROWED

L'Chaim

We wed beneath
the chuppah
snowy linen dusting
your forehead,
children holding hands,
recess under monkey bars.
The ring is vintage
a gift from my grandmother
widowed young
you kiss me hard

& shatter glass
into chunks.

Earl Grey

A fall & a whack
We are old
Waking cats &
Stretch to the kitchen to see
An old china set
Your grandmother met
With a matching
Now smashed, pot of tea

We tidy the mess
A marital test
The feline is hiding away
We search & search
When we find she is perched
Professing "it is all a mistake"

The rain is loud & the
Cat quite proud
As she bats a sliver of bone
So we curl back to sleep as
I kiss your heartbeat
Blood pumping life into stone

Vesuvius

The hike is steep
with distractions like
tiny huts packed with Italian trinkets &
beautiful, wrinkled Napolitano women.
I am 8 months pregnant
draped in a thin muslin frock, my belly swollen
like a ripe l'anguria.
I climb

& climb
like the Guggenheim
as earth coats my toes
near the top of the world where
dust floats by in copper clouds.

But you are my Jack
& fetch water
as I come stumbling
through the cramped shop
to buy a bottle of cold limoncello
which we uncork in a
New Jersey hospital
as soon as I erupt.

Wheels

Sippy cups in tow, we three bound
down the sidewalk in our shiny
side by side,
plush & pink with plaid upholstery
a sleek dashboard
silver rims & a standard bumper
which the barefoot daughters
kick as they shower crackers
into each other's hair.
We roll right through
that bakery door wedged open
with a hunk of wood.
The daughters salivate as
buttery flakes
fly from bread & cakes
crumbs dance in wicker baskets,

we choose a morning glory

& idle in the sun.

Salt Between Us

Lazurite sky, you plod in, children plunge
on your sunburned back & giggle.

A seagull pecks on a scab of crust.

Family is distant now, splotches
bobbing along cobalt waves I wave them in.

We feast on soggy sandwiches, dented
fruit, dribbles of crimson drip as a breeze
flips your page

you fumble with the chapter, suck
the pit of a plum.

Sticky & dripping the daughters
are melting like ice pops,
so you amble one small hand

in each of yours
to the mouth of our momentary inlet
& splash.

The Spy Who Loved Me

Sometimes you are a little like 007. That is when
I feast on you like

Pussy Galore. You snake & whoosh winter slopes
alongside a Shirley Bassey serenade

charcoal trousers, grey
wooly cap & a beautiful burning stick

you manage to keep lit
as you plow over moguls, skate between trees

grin thin as Bond villains shoot & spin
through snowy flakes   you stay cool, slicing silver

Rossignols into powder, glancing back quick to study
the bad guys only to see

your small daughters attempting to keep up
with their dad,

snow plowing in peach ski pants
& blue wobbly helmets.

New June

The town pool splashes
with half-naked dysfunction.
Kids in pink hats
& mint crocs skittle by young
moms as they flip-flop
to the parking lot, straw bags swing
like empty briefcases.
Earbud-clad, gaggles of tweenagers swagger by
manicured & pedicured, American Girl dolls
in white bikinis.

This is where they learned to swim,
gliding & flying through cerulean water,
wet mops squeezed into latex caps, ferocious limbs
smacking behind,
our miniature tsunamis, bronze arms
cascading under shadows of backstroke flags

waving like summer leaves
cheering on our lithe Pisces, as they flip & twist
under soft waves of youth.

Mechanics

Even in the dark English dawn
mechanics begin as your father
navigates dim lit hallways,
crown of snow in charcoal grey,
he loads the boot while we gulp
cold tea & hug your mum
in that garden
where wellies weave through
wisteria & small
shovels sleep on a sunny slab
flecks of mud & rubble,
broad beans sleep in a bowl but

bustle has begun
doors swing open
bags are lifted & wheeled

Beep

        Beep

                Beep

You tie my shoe, I clutch my passport
he walks us in before goodbye
currant pastries, black coffee
a crowded wonderful crumb filled table,

this will be the last time.

Laden with stuff
you hobble toward the gate,
lap-belts buckle as you
close your eyes
silently admiring the man
forever making things work.

Hiss

Each time we reach
a month without sex
I book a meal over candlelight,
finally
perhaps,
prelude to a fuck.
We hold hands to the car, your
palm strong in my grip as
Autumn rain pelts our toes.

The house is chilled as we
amble in, daughters need a bath,
cat laps oil from an open box,
mozzarella clings to the carpet like Crest
across the counter. I carve & dig
with a dull knife
you liberate hot water from rusted pipes
& retreat alone.

Hunt

I strain spaghetti, hum a song
we used to sing when
I see it vanish
slip through a ripped screen
I'll never mend.
My apron hangs loose, straps sway like our
daughters' ponytails, I dash
into a garden where weeds sprout from
cavernous hollows, deeply I
forage through dandelion tangles,
a small girl hunting for the afikoman.
As in prayer back in my kitchen
I flip through lids, thump through clutter,
thumb through scribbled recipes, oak tag
splattered with generations of mettle. I even
rummage through the recycling bin
where sharp glass snags my thumb

& notice it
snoozing beneath ash.
So I carry the little tray like a holy relic
to dissect the fragments
salvage what is left but it is dust
& disintegrates
the wind, panting.
Now shrouded in wet grey light, I dump
the dinner
overcooked pasta like coagulated flesh
surrender & listen
to the sky howl.

Embers

Our union flakes like dead skin
we rub aloe, we sit in shade, we
buy a house
in the Catskill mountains
built of stone & cordwood
strong square windows
red door, smooth black
pond where frogs & toads
sing in the muddy
night & marshmallows
roast on brittle branches.

There is a glow
when you slouch by a fire
smile a little, wave a butt, sip
whisky from a paper
cup. The daughters smile &
together you build s'mores
gobs of gelatin
slip between fingers
& plop into a
dying hearth.

Repair

The shop stems
from a narrow Newark street
where garages cram together like
broken Legos,
we dine with plastic forks on the hood
of a half-painted Subaru
devour pan-seared
scallops, spanish potatoes,
a twisted spine of geranium
leans into the heat,
beer is cold.
I flower a little
when I'm near rotting transmissions
tarnished rims, greasy
men under decaying carriages.
       Later,
when all things beautiful
        wither
I discover the petals, parched
under a dark window
        & lend them sun.

BLUE

Shadows

Your easel
still slants here
overlooks our pond
roiled with mud
tubes of used blues left scattered
in damp weeds
bleed into earth
where it seems you
crouch on a sailcloth stool
gliding a badger's bristles
over canvas.

Mass

She spits into our draped
cell yanks the curtains
behind her they wave
like pale sheets
just before thunder, short
sharp like a paring knife
the doc keeps carving that word
chiseling it into his
lungs, engraving it against
the chambers of our heart.

Diagnosis

I flash to the darkness
how it buries us
press bare knees to chest cry
sponge my snot
tiptoe to the kitchen grab a bottle
yesterday's coffee mug
quick rinse
pour

wine is warm
I drink anyway
dry floral hues tickle my throat as
I stare at recipe cards
& cartons of cereal
yank a drawer, stack pens in piles
alphabetize the spice rack

anise
       black pepper
              cloves

scrub a burnt pan
until fingers are raw
fill a teapot.

Walls are quiet but for your breath
clogged vacuum hose,
I kneel &
stare at my newness born
as the kettle cries.

Closer

June
We always take the furthest spot,
eager to walk
the flat expanse of the parking lot.
On occasion you smile in those first days
swollen with hope,
late June sunshine on your shoulders,
Dogwood just in bloom.

August
Hot, you wave a limp wrist
motioning me to park nearer.
The tree is laden with green now
like emerald stars. Ghosts float
through glass doors that clunk
shut behind.

November
You hobble from car to lobby
filled with mums & pumpkins.
That wool cap fits loose now, your face still
beautiful,
chiseled, sunken.

February
Carrying your bag
I walk near to a nurse who
wheels your chair
through an infusion room where
I have morphed
seemingly, into Simon of Cyrene.

Stages

1.   Fastened
like a toddler, your co-driver shouts instructions,
directions
hurtling harmonies of
roar, mud & smut.

2.   We watch through
drizzle, fog & fumes cheer as you steer
beyond grizzled
twigs & amputated
branches.

3.   But you hit &
a copter spirals like that scene from Miss Saigon,
above two small girls
wrapped in red macs
ripe with that possibility.

4.   It is over now.
But you still hurtle toward us, silhouette
against sunshine
under variegated halos
of light.

Dawn at the Station

Sunday is soft here, cement
freshly swept like marble countertops
silver stones stand
indifferent along the ballast
like faces in a subway car.

Grackles, early morning flight
glides black against billows
speckled sparrows land on
tousled branches as a train
pelts placid like a billiard

cue over baize, bodies
scramble off the platform
like nearly swatted
flies, my fingers are bored I rub
pens in pockets.

Busy now, the rails shriek like
hydraulic cutlery machines
I hasten my gait breath like brume,
steam in an engine.

Therapy

Weekly I sweep past
the living, they
chase futures
down jammed
sidewalks. Therapy is

feeble
a stack from a time with
magazines,
a tank lined with pebbles, one
large lone goldfish
orange like an
American president.

Now her name her space
sheds from memory,
slim room walls
like vanilla wafers,
my suede boots wet
from a time when
Manhattan had
snow.

We suck
chamomile from styrofoam
as she listens
to me bitch
until that soft
tone of her phone
my cue to smear my tears &
cloak, once again,
against the elements.

Ride

The drive is onerous, congested
cars beep & bellow,
trapped beneath the Hudson.

Vested now in an exclusive club
I stroll into Sloan, nod to the jolly concierge
swoop a handful of Lifesavers from a dainty tray

you hobble behind
sadly at home now in this "members only"
circled by bent men & silver women.

The wait is always long, your face gaunt
& raw, a tired finger rests against an
image on your phone

dented metal against a
summer bronze sky
clay splattered on your blue race-suit.

Mourning

My limp beige bra, your torn suede slippers,
pink viles, violet pills, pots of vomit,
pools of vaseline in lids.

I rub jelly into fresh bed sores
tuck our soft afghan,
stripes of tangerine & tomato
under damp skin
sweep sweats of pewter hair
from your forehead
& fall asleep, a dog
by your feet, until
morning.

Last First Night

I pose we smoke
that joint fun we
still partake in

but
7 becomes 8
8 becomes 9
you are still
on the other side
of the locked door,
Ursus in hibernation.

So I mark time
mull red wine
with cardamom
& lemon peel
pour the spirit
into porcelain
teacups & pass
to my teenage children,
late popsicles
on a summer night.

At 11:55 you appear
your once strong body
fading with the year
you hobble a few steps
in striped pajamas,
that Jew from Treblinka
watching Anderson Cooper.

I graze your shoulder,
strands of
your damp hair
too weak to inhale
you peck me instead
with chapped lips as
your last year begins.

Clan

We listen to *Clan of the Cave Bear*
as I drive the tribe to our
house in the woods &
sit by some kindling with
the daughters
wrapped in wool.

The tumors hasten through
your bones now
but somehow still strong
you carry my hand
to an otter's holt where
broken leaves shuffle like
crushed capsules under boots.

From a distance,
we hear happy chatter
as apricot flames stretch
toward the stars
the daughters craft the pyre just as
you taught them
tilt logs together
like the tent we pitched
& crawled into,
barefoot newlyweds.

Shit

I avoid the bowels of our house,
a pit with boxes & bicycles
where my cats piss
in litter & skitter across scars, but today,
six days before you die,

the scent is rancid so
I pounce down to tackle the smelly plastic box
piled high with feline turds like seesaws
but instead find three obliterated pipes, brown swill
spilling like Katrina, quick I slosh around desperate to salvage
piles unremembered
but slop oozes fast & the scooping begins.

Marlboro Man

In those last days
when you could only whisper
you said, "I have a hankering
for a fag."

That delicious
bleached tobacco leaf
rolled & tucked
between your fingers.

So I held it to your lips
lit with a soft blue BIC
so you could be a man
once more.

Pasteur Pipette

Just a swaddled shroud
you lay dying
on that mechanical monster
still snarling
in our living
room
between
songs of quietus
I drip love
into your
open mouth.

Zipper

Our curtain opens to a
brittle February dawn

two strangers in
lab coats

like milkmen in
Pleasantville

a quick long zip
our daughters' coats in winter.

Half Moon

Sleep soft on half a moon with me, my love,
Cradle me tight deep within your crescent;
Where even stars stare, jealous from above.
Fuck me in blackness until we are spent
High above the heat of an angry sun;
Where reality's light cannot find us,
We will feast in peace on our fine fortune.
I touch your eyes & lick your lids in lust.
But the moon must grow, plump into a sphere
Our fingers claw the surface as we slip;
A Chagall, weightless, over clouds & tears;
My head on your heart, my curls on your lip.
      We kiss hard as we plummet into earth,
      & weep whilst we face this jolting rebirth.

NEW

Widow

A no-nonsense Fern Arable
she chops heads off chickens
feathers flap like banners in the breeze as
blood drains & squirts from severed skin.
Ignoring the gore she throws slop to hogs,
stomping around the muddy pen

in his boots, sweating like
only a woman does
she carries that evening's water to the
farmhouse, wooden buckets, like scales of justice,
slope leaden against her back.

Wintertide

Ice cracks in tandem with wind
a still, dark pond, dead weeds
preserved
suspended in chilled breath.

I sit cross-legged on flat rock like the
slate near my grandfather's creek where
I paddled & played with my sister,
my cousins
barefoot, splashing,
scooping slimy fish into nets
like some Norman Rockwell painting.

A hawk skates through these
mountain trees capped in flurry
like shredded coconut on
pistachio,

below frogs lie dormant
pond-bottom in fogs of glop,
water striders
wintering deep inside stems
as wolves fill the nightfall.

Kin

I lounge
on the judge's lawn like
we did

boiling hot dogs & sliding
midsummer marshmallows
onto bent twigs,
cushions blue beyond
us scattered
like the day's sky.

The kids play
chase like chipmunks under
waltzing leaves as we
snap nachos & drink
Pinot Noir, naked toes
in each other's laps.

As the fire dies I couple with
her King Charles Spaniel
he laps my nose,
I scratch his ear & lean my twig
up against theirs.

Prison

The daughter's permit allows her passage to the DMV
where teenagers road test under the glare of
East Jersey State. Where decaying gardens skirt
deteriorating Victorians & chainlinks scintillate
beneath a blue-collar sun.

Where the state plopped a prison complete with
barracks like brick limbs at Birkenau,
strong arms reaching for something
other than this.

Thanksgiving

Cranberries melt in the pan, tears
bubbling over flame.
I peel pale wrinkled parsnips
fizzle the flesh in oil, chop onions & crack
eggs into matzo meal, cadaverous balls float
like eyeballs in this witch's brew.

The table
is set for three
silverware on tawny placemats,
a lone wine stem, I sip him
insist my parents
not break bread with us
this year,

we sit silent
occasional mention
of the cats
turkey is dry, gravy
is cold & a store-bought cake
sweats on the counter.

Plus None

They congratulate
themselves, speeches for various mitzvot
beaded bags swing with presumption.

Couples fasten to buddies
like that kindergarten trip to the zoo.
My feeble red

attempts to mingle
all fancy
in her wine glass, I unfold

a paper smile, devour
three deviled eggs, flaxen yolks
whipped like vanilla sundaes.

The table is plated for seven. I polite
a nod to the panel over
a centerpiece of pink tulips

three couples deliberate over
babysitters, supermarkets,
toy shops. The flowers

peer from center, I stare back,
note the petals are also in pairs
& leave.

Pretending

I burrow into his scrub
a mongoose
instinctively navigating
complex tunnels to
lie in the lowlands
of dirt & darkness
hiding my wilds.
I feed on his
lips, his dick. He cups
my head,
ringlets twirl about
his fingers. Giddy,
we twirl across his mattress
like an Edwardian picnic
under an English summer
with you.

Black Pudding

I borrow Christmas
as it isn't mine to keep.
Mincemeat stuffed into pastry
brandy butter,
pudding frantic in flame doused
in cognac
the muddy fruit scooped amongst

cheers in a dim room as
I pass my crock to your mum
her long neck
perched in a raspberry scarf
& consume.

Fall Risk

Kart I wake
Drunken state
Hair knot funk
Like kid punk
Reek of piss
Band slaps wrist
Doze on gurney
Slow dark journey

Have to sow, have to reap
No time to stop, no time to sleep

      So I YANK off these tethers
like our mothers burned their bras
& strut green-gowned
into terror.

Camphor

Shivering I squirm face up
on a brumal metal bed
wand shifts deep within my pit.
Her face slices a slip of pity as she orders me to
contort my arm high above my head,
gel warms my chest as
I flash to my grandmother's camphor oil,
more computer clicks,
the DOCTOR has arrived.

Transferred to a second
room, pink-robed
chair in a corner, little Jack Horner
I wait
check my texts
fiddle with bracelets, twirl the curls
of my hair, blow my nose
the clock pounds, finally a white coat hurries in with

      mass

tumor

      growth

stage

vectors aimed at my tits exactly like they were
at my children's father's lungs sixteen months ago.

He is dead.

Leaves

Now, I sit on a stone wall, sad
like Humpty Dumpty
paddle miles over paths of mud
skeletal remains of leaves left dead
to stamp, tromp, tramp on soil's crust
hybridized with a tree's innards.

Garden State

They buzz me in. Washed walls,
cobalt bowls, patterned pipes.
A high-smiling apothecary
gifts me three glass jars of pungent flower
like the lilies on our wedding day.

Road Test

My bag gapes while I dig.
DMV with the daughter,
17 today,

license, registration, insurance, ma'am

I find it!

Minivan reeks of sweat, pretzels &
swim team towels, center console bursts with
pennies, keys, a few crumpled dollar bills,

insurance is stale.

The daughter is instructed to return next week
(when her mother gets her shit together)
so she pulls to the curb & decisively jams
that magic wand into

Drive.

Songbirds

Christmas is over
but conifers still
twinkle like pellucid salt specks
on sidewalks. I am 50 today
and wake to the warble of
lemon goldfinch
& cherry cardinal, they poke
seed from dead blossoms their
slim clementine beaks stab at
twisted vines & fly into infinity.

I savor this morning's coffee,
crusted brown sugar
dissolves as my little spoon spins
round & round
echoes
fluttering.

Butcher

They run giggling with the little cousin
into a blue room lined with
death & freezers.
The kids take no notice of
refrigerated flesh
necks, breasts & thighs
neatly dressed in pressed cellophane,
instead they
carry on a game of
hide & seek amongst
tendon & bone.

Soon, bored & cold
they shiver ridiculous
like the last survivors of an Alaskan plane crash,
grandmother shushes them
checks her wallet & chucks two more
headless, wrapped in plastic.
At checkout the cousin
requests candy. A plastic
pickle tub is presented
filled with cherry goldfish, lemon
lollipops & pink bubble gum.
We skip out,
our family, holding hands, mouths
stuffed with sugar.

Kosher

Like me, the surgical nurse
is freckled, chestnut hair, slim
in loose fitting
pink scrubs. He tucks
my curls under a mint paper cap,
white tubes like vacuum hoses are
unraveled & assigned.
Screens
   BEEP
      FLASH
& wave. I am
a beige slab under
a warm white blanket
staff shuffle in & out of
my cute curtained purgatory puncturing
my veins with needles with smiles,
scoot me into a chilled room to scrape away
this malady, toss cancered flesh into the trash
like rotten sausages.

Diaphanous

For Chloë & Sophie

Ferns and spiders
sunbathe in slim open
window where light cuts in like lemon
slices across her patchwork quilt
the daughters perch on a mustard-draped bed
dandelion hair in denim flares
they sketch & sing,
where I tiptoe on occasion
deep into their magical room
like some character in a
Roald Dahl book, my little
Miss Honeys lay flat stacks
of crisp paper & delicate knolls of flaxen
glitter glides on a breeze like fairy dust.

Trash

All haze the
air we sip the
strangers
we fuck

steam, cumulus
over the bowery.
I jump on his back
my whore-heeled sandals dangle
unbuckled above a spate of
fresh black trash bags like sea-polished stones,

slipping, he anchors me
I kiss the swanskin
of his nape deep beneath
a smudged sky.

Sideways

Sometimes I bitch
to him
when it's about me, toss
my shit from suitcase to bed instead of
tucking tidy like origami
into corners.
Sometimes I fuck some husk
but twist to him, my tongue in
some throat
like a cherry popsicle.
Sometimes I mislay the hotel
key, treasure
buried under sheets.
Sometimes I slant my billow
through the slice from his city
window, clouds
sneaking back in to bite.
And sometimes we talk
until daylight wanes,
when I sprawl across
his chest bestrewn
with my curls,
ribbons on a gift.

Pacifier

The tick of ceiling blades
lull my synthetic breasts to sleep.

I swaddle the new mounds
like you did, when you were alive

shrouding the girls & soothing them
with pink rubber binkys.

Thread

I still fuck your shirts to sleep
widowed skin
against Egyptian cotton,
crisp blue stripes rub my chest
black buttons stroke my breasts
until
that
damn tag

jabs
      jabs
            Jabs
at my nape
like a telegraph message from
the war department I turn to
yank but
STOP
It is your name
stitched in fine black thread,
silk woven cobweb.

Play Date

I lay damp
draped in cream lace
sweat seeps into cotton sheets,
little pools
under newly constructed

tits like lunch pail ice packs
the dampness trails
spine to coccyx, I touch
body's thirst
sweep to my inner thigh
where I find myself.

Blue Jeans

Eventually, I clean, pick up after you
once more
dead Levi's scattered in lumps along the
earth of your closet like
crumpled drugstore receipts.

I count six &
whip each, microscopic specks of
dust fly from the denim, bits of you
in my hair & my face.

I fold, dote on each
bend, pleat, line
waistband to cuff,
run fingers over dark
spots in pigment, smoothing cloth
into tidy squares like

postage stamps, I wish to lick
& stick on a
self-addressed envelope
so you come back.

ACKNOWLEDGEMENTS

Thanks to the editors of the following publications in which versions of some of these poems first appeared:

"Blue Jeans": *The Comstock Review*
"Closer": *Scarlet Leaf Review*
"Cuffs": *Eunoia Review*
"Diagnosis": *Neuron Walker*
"Diaphanous": *Flora Fiction*
"Fringes": *Cliterature*
"Last First Night" & "Leaves": *Vita Brevis Press*
"Mourning": *Dream Noir*
"Mourning": *Better Than Starbucks*
"New June": *Brief Wilderness*
"Pasteur Pipette": *Pain & Renewal Anthology*
"Repair": *Broad River Review*
"Therapy": *Black Fox Literary Review*
"Trash": *Horror Sleaze Trash*

Deepest love to my family: *Mark CG Lawrence*, Chloë Frances Lawrence, Sophie Catherine Lawrence, Barbara Bader Zeichner, Charles Zeichner & Jodi Zeichner Raditz.

I will always remember & be grateful for the support of Nikki Giovanni, Catherine Doty, BJ Ward, Ras Heru Stewart & Ted Rall.

Thank you to my doctors & their dedicated staffs for saving me: Diana Addis, Konika Bose, Charles Ciolino, Amy Dimun, Mary Hunt, Peter Hyans, Amber Khan, Lauren Im-Imamru, Jesse Mangone, Lisa Mills, Erika Pietzsch, Lyubov Shkarupa, Hugh Snyder & Jennifer Lublin.

Thank you to the people of The Writer's Circle. Thank you to the people of The Robert Frost House. Thank you to the people of the Edna St. Vincent Millay Colony & Thank you to Peter Murphy & his magical poetry circles.

Cheers to stories & to those, living & *dead*, who helped to fuel them: JD Ackley, *Frances Bader*, Ivan Bader, Jean Bader, *Samuel Bader*, Arnoldo Barrantes, Therman Brown, Theresa Burns, James Butler, Patricia Canning, Robert

Cardonsky, CHS Department of English, Ian Clark, Terence Dalton, Mia DeGioia, Ellen Dreyer, Brenda Ehlers, Abi Erhamza, Kara Erhamza, Levent Erhamza, *Catherine Fairbairns, Anthony Fairbairns*, Maria Gaines, Ari Kalish, Brett Kalish, Hope Kalish, Jared Kalish, Larry Kalish, Eric Klein, Amy Koehler, Ethan Koehler, Don Lasko, Dora Lawrence, Elliot Lawrence, FH Lawrence, Frederick Lawrence, *Garth Lawrence*, Henri Lawrence, *Jinx Lawrence*, Marta Lawrence, *Maggie Lawrence, Milton Lawrence, Mortimer Lawrence*, Nancy Lawrence, Neil Lawrence, *Nona Lawrence*, Paolo Lawrence, *Roxanne Lawrence*, Valerie Lawrence, Peter Licata, Ned Lindsay, Shana Lindsay, Robert Macjiewski, Willie Mack, Sherri Manning, Constantine Mantopoulos, *Larry McKim, David Milton-Hall*, Michael Novemsky, Nimfa Oliviero, Kena Onyejekwe, Annie Pasternak, Marc Peeters, Adam Raditz, Drew Raditz, Zoe Raditz, *Yvonne Rall*, Jonathan Rose, Adam Rothenberg, Christie Rothenberg, Laura Russo, Stacey Salem-Antonucci, Nicole Sonneblick, Scott Stantis, Jocelyn Torres, Anne Wessel, Alana West, Khadijah White, Robert Young, Janice Zeichner, Saul Zeichner, *Joseph Zeichner, Sally Zeichner* & Jennifer Almario Dalton.

And a final thank you to the students of Columbia High School from whom I learn year after year.

Photo Credits: Chloë Frances Lawrence, Ethan Koehler, Frederick Lawrence, Sophie Catherine Lawrence
Proofreader: Barbara Bader Zeichner

A young widow and cancer survivor, **Stacey Z Lawrence** is a veteran public high school teacher of Poetry, Creative Writing & Drama. Her work can be seen in *The Comstock Review, Eunoia Review, Flora Fiction, Broad River Review, Vita Brevis, Dream Noir* & others. She was both long & short-listed for the 2019 & 2021 Fish Prize in Poetry, judged by Billy Collins. Stacey has a BA in Drama from William Paterson University, an MA in English & MAT in Speech & Theater from Montclair State University & was awarded a fellowship to the Robert Frost House in 2016. She was a coach & mentor for the national PoetryOutLoud competition & the NJ Governor's Awards. Stacey co-founded the drama company Stage Right Productions & was director of the social action performance troupe Impact Theater. In 2012 she worked with playwright Naomi Patz to direct the debut production of Karel Svenk's devastating Holocaust parody, *The Last Cyclist*. She is the creator of student programs The Write Stuff & Write in the Wood & the former lead singer of the bands, Test Pattern & Three In Motion. An avid hiker, Stacey has a writing cottage in the Catskill mountains. She is the mother of 2 incredible daughters & 4 cool cats. *Fall Risk* is her first book.

CPSIA information can be obtained
at www.ICGtesting.com
Printed in the USA
BVHW062117040921
615735BV00004B/20

9 781646 625697